NATIONAL GEOGRAPHIC KiDS

DOGGY DEFENDERS

WILLOW

★ ★ ★

THE THERAPY DOG

Lisa M. Gerry
Photographs by Lori Epstein

NATIONAL GEOGRAPHIC
WASHINGTON, D.C.

Meet
WILLOW!

Willow is a rescued greyhound. Greyhounds have long bodies and pointy snouts, which help them run really fast.

She lives with her best friend, Megan.

Willow loves to relax
at home and **nap.**

But she also works
really hard: She has a job!

Willow is a therapy dog.

She knows how to make people smile and helps them feel better if they are sad.

Every morning, Willow gets ready for work. Her good friend Jim helps her get dressed.

Willow wears a **bright red vest to** let people know that she is a therapy dog.

Every day on the job is different for Willow.

Today, she is going to visit a hospital.

Inside the hospital, Megan and Willow join some more of their friends: other therapy dogs!

They all work together to help sick people feel better.

Willow and her friends visit the patients.

Willow is very gentle.

She lies close so people can pet her.

Willow makes people smile.

Great job, Willow.

Willow also visits the **doctors** and **nurses** to thank them for their hard work.

They love seeing Willow!

Now it's time for
Willow's next visit.

Willow and Megan are going to visit a **school**. There, Willow will help the busy students feel happy and relaxed.

Everyone gives Willow
kisses and hugs.

She brings big smiles
to their faces.

Next, Willow and Megan head to a home for retired veterans.

Veterans are people who have served in the military.

They pet Willow's soft fur and scratch behind her ears.

Willow has brightened their day.

Now Willow and Megan
have one more stop to make.
They are visiting a library!

Willow will help kids
practice reading.

The kids
love reading to
Willow. She is a
great listener!

Phew, what a long day—now it's time to **relax!** Willow spends her free time making new friends ...

Willow

... snacking on special treats ...

... and cuddling!

But even when she's not working, Willow doesn't stop making people smile.

She makes Jim smile. She makes Megan smile. And they make her smile, too!

Now, after a long day and lots of fun, it's time for bed. Megan helps Willow put on her pajamas.

Good night, Willow!
Thank you for helping.

Meet the Team!

Megan answers questions about Willow and helping their community.

Q How did you get Willow?

A I adopted Willow from Second Chance Greyhounds (SCG), a greyhound rescue organization located in Georgia. SCG finds homes for former racing greyhounds.

Q Who trained Willow?

A Willow learned basic skills with Second Chance Greyhounds. We passed the AKC Canine Good Citizen test and then we became a certified therapy team with People. Animals. Love. (PAL).

Q What do you and Willow do in your free time?

A Willow and I love to go for car rides together and play upbeat music—Willow looks out the windows and bobs her head to the music. She also enjoys going out to eat with me and her dog sister, Pumpkin.

Q **What is Willow's favorite toy?**

A Willow has a big stuffed dog named Uga that she cuddles and sleeps on during the afternoon. She also likes to take my shoes—not to chew them but to sleep with them.

Q **What is the best part of owning a therapy dog?**

A I love experiencing the amazing and unique ability that animals have to heal people. It's a blessing to see and feel while watching Willow working.

Willow's Tips on Being a Good Friend and Neighbor

Willow works hard to make people happy. Here's how you can help make people smile, too!

1. **Volunteer! Ask a parent to help you spend time with a local charity or group.**

2. **Be there for your friends and loved ones when they need it.**

3. **Talk, share, and listen to friends and family.**

4. **Respect others: Respect people and your differences.**

5. **Always ask permission before approaching or petting a dog.**

6. **Use your manners: Say please and thank you.**

7. **If you are getting a pet, try adopting one from a shelter.**

8. **Donate the toys and books you don't want anymore.**

Published by National Geographic Partners, LLC. All rights reserved. Reproduction of the whole or any part of the contents without written permission from the publisher is prohibited.

Since 1888, the National Geographic Society has funded more than 12,000 research, exploration, and preservation projects around the world. The Society receives funds from National Geographic Partners, LLC, funded in part by your purchase. A portion of the proceeds from this book supports this vital work. To learn more, visit natgeo.com/info.

NATIONAL GEOGRAPHIC and Yellow Border Design are trademarks of the National Geographic Society, used under license.

For more information, visit nationalgeographic.com, call 1-877-873-6846, or write to the following address:

National Geographic Partners
1145 17th Street N.W.
Washington, D.C. 20036-4688 U.S.A.

Visit us online at nationalgeographic.com/books
For librarians and teachers: nationalgeographic.com /books/librarians-and-educators/
More for kids from National Geographic: natgeokids.com

National Geographic Kids magazine inspires children to explore their world with fun yet educational articles on animals, science, nature, and more. Using fresh story-telling and amazing photography, *Nat Geo Kids* shows kids ages 6 to 14 the fascinating truth about the world— and why they should care.
kids.nationalgeographic.com/subscribe

For information about special discounts for bulk pur-chases, please contact National Geographic Books Special Sales: specialsales@natgeo.com

For rights or permissions inquiries, please contact National Geographic Books Subsidiary Rights: bookrights@natgeo.com

Designed by Callie Broaddus

The publisher would like to thank Lisa Gerry, author; Lori Epstein, photographer; Paige Towler, project editor; Shannon Hibberd, photo editor; and Willow, Megan, Jim, George Washington University Hospital, Lt. Joseph P. Kenney Institute, Garfield Elementary School, Armed Forces Retirement Home, PAL (People. Animals. Love.), Mt. Pleasant Library, and Hero Dogs for their support and dedication to their communities.

Library of Congress Cataloging-in-Publication Data
 Names: Gerry, Lisa, author.
 Title: Willow the rescue dog / by Lisa M. Gerry.
 Description: Washington, DC : National Geographic Kids, [2019] | Series: Doggy defenders | Audience: Ages 4-8. | Audience: K to grade 3.
 Identifiers: LCCN 2018031630| ISBN 9781426334474 (hardcover) | ISBN 9781426334481 (hardcover)
 Subjects: LCSH: Rescue dogs—Juvenile literature. | Dogs— Therapeutic use—Juvenile literature. | Human-animal relationships—Juvenile literature.
 Classification: LCC SF426.5 .G47 2019 | DDC 636.7/0886—dc23
 LC Record available at https://lccn.loc.gov/2018031630

Printed in the United States of America
19/WOR/2